TECHNOLOGY AT WORK

AT THE
AIRPORT

Richard Spilsbury

Raintree
Chicago, Illinois

Designed by Richard Parker and Tinstar Design Ltd
Illustrations by Darren Lingard
Printed and bound in China by CTPS

13 12 11 10 09
10 9 8 7 6 5 4 3 2 1

Library of Congress Cataloging-in-Publication Data
Spilsbury, Richard, 1963-
  At the airport / Richard Spilsbury.
      p. cm. -- (Technology at work)
  Includes bibliographical references and index.
  ISBN 978-1-4109-3175-7 (hc)
  1. Aeronautics--Juvenile literature. 2. Airports--Juvenile literature. I. Title.
  TL547.S7178 2008
  387.7--dc22
                                2008005440

Acknowledgments
The publishers would like to thank the following for permission to reproduce photographs: ©Alamy /
Stock Connection Blue p. **24**; ©A1 Pix Limited p. **28**; ©BAA Limited pp. **5**, **6**, **9**, **12-13**, **16**, **21**, **23**, **26-27**,
29; ©Corbis pp. **17** (Thinkstock), **18** (Imageshop); ©CTI Systems p. **20**.

Cover photograph of X-ray of bag, reproduced with permission of ©Getty Images (The Image Bank).

Every effort has been made to contact copyright holders of any material reproduced in this book. Any
omissions will be rectified in subsequent printings if notice is given to the publishers.

We would like to thank Ian Graham for his invaluable help in the preparation of this book.

Disclaimer
All the internet addresses (URLs) given in this book were valid at time of going to press. However, due
to the dynamic nature of the Internet, some addresses may have changed, or sites may have changed
or ceased to exist since publication. While the author and publishers regret any inconvenience this
may cause readers, no responsibility for any such changes can be accepted by either the author or the
publishers. It is recommended that adults supervise children on the Internet.

CONTENTS

Some words are printed in bold, **like this**. You can find out what they mean by looking in the glossary.

WHAT IS AN AIRPORT?

An airport is a place where **aircraft** take off and land. Aircraft pick up or drop off passengers and their luggage. Passengers are the people transported by a vehicle. Aircraft also transport **cargo** such as boxes of food, toys, shoes, or televisions.

Parts of the airport

The main building at an airport is called the **terminal**. Many people work in the terminal. Companies called airlines sell tickets for flights here. The airline staff organizes who and what goes on each airplane. The terminal is also the place where people wait. Passengers waiting to leave on an airplane sit in the departure lounge or wait at the departure gate. Friends or family of passengers who are due to arrive on airplanes wait in the arrival lounge or wait at the arrival gate.

The other parts of an airport are outside. The **apron** is the area where aircraft are emptied of passengers and cargo and prepared for another flight. The **runway** is the strip of ground on which airplanes take off and land.

AT WORK

BUSIEST TERMINAL

Roughly 85 million people use the Atlanta airport terminal each year. Nearly 1 million takeoffs and landings happen there every year.

Airports are busy places. Passengers wait for their flights inside the terminal, while aircraft take off and land outside.

CHECK-IN

At the airport check-in desk, passengers show their tickets and identification to airline staff. They check luggage and packages to go in the **hold** of the airplane. Thousands of people check in each day. So how do airlines know which luggage belongs to which passenger, and on which airplane it goes?

Bar codes and stripes

Check-in workers attach a different bar code to each piece of luggage. The bar code links the bag to information about the passenger and flight held in the airline's computer system.

Each piece of luggage has its own individual bar code to identify it.

How bar code readers work

Luggage handlers use handheld bar code readers to read the code on a bag before loading it onto an airplane. These **machines** use light to read bar codes because light reflects back more from white spaces than black bars. By using bar code readers, luggage handlers can sort luggage very quickly.

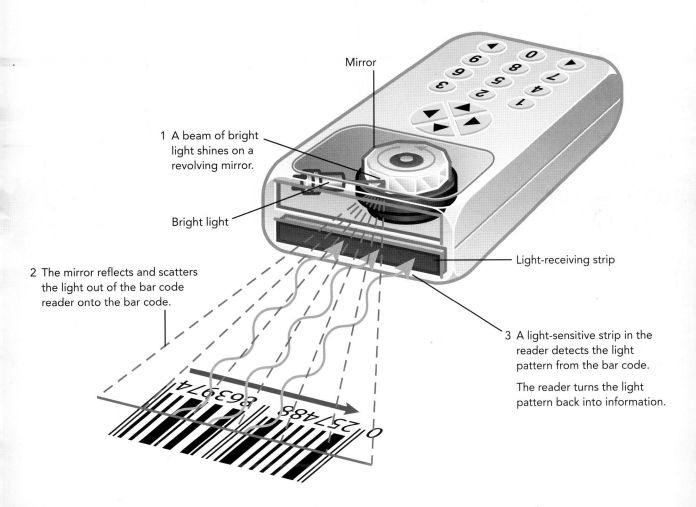

Mirror

1 A beam of bright light shines on a revolving mirror.

Bright light

2 The mirror reflects and scatters the light out of the bar code reader onto the bar code.

Light-receiving strip

3 A light-sensitive strip in the reader detects the light pattern from the bar code.

The reader turns the light pattern back into information.

KEEPING SECURE

Airport **terminals** are very busy places. Terminals are sometimes targets for criminals who want to cause damage to the building or to **aircraft**. Airport **security** workers make sure airports are safe for everyone to use.

Searching for danger

Workers open some hand luggage that will be taken onto airplanes. They search for any weapons or objects, such as cigarette lighters, that could be dangerous if taken onto an airplane. They also use **machines** to help them search for danger. Metal detectors are machines that can detect knives and other metal objects hidden in people's clothes.

AT WORK

USING MAGNETS TO FIND METAL

A compass needle points north because it can detect a **magnetic field** made by the Earth. A magnetic field is the area around a **magnet** where objects are affected by magnetic **forces**. A metal detector uses electricity to make its own magnetic field. The magnetic field changes when something made of metal comes near it. A metal detector beeps when the field changes.

Passengers often forget to remove metal jewelry and empty coins from their pockets before going through a metal detector. If the alarm is set off, passengers need to be inspected by security.

LOOKING INSIDE

It would take too much time for airport **security** workers to open every piece of hand luggage and search for anything dangerous. If this happened, passengers would probably miss their flights. Instead workers put all hand luggage on a conveyer belt. This passes the luggage through a **scanner**. The scanner looks inside using X-rays, and shows the contents of the luggage on a screen. Workers can then tell whether or not anything dangerous is in the luggage.

What is an X-ray?

X-rays are invisible rays or beams of **energy**. They can pass through anything soft, such as plastic or flesh, but they bounce back off things that are hard, such as bone or metal. X-rays are also used in hospitals to see whether bones are broken. X-ray technology was discovered in 1895.

IN THE FUTURE

Millimeter-wave scanners will soon be able to look through clothes and create images of anything carried under a person's clothes, whether it is made of metal, plastic, or other materials.

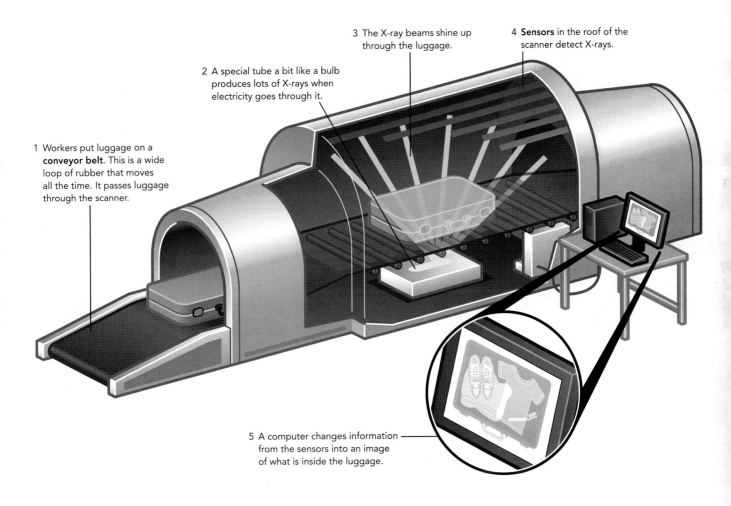

3 The X-ray beams shine up through the luggage.

4 **Sensors** in the roof of the scanner detect X-rays.

2 A special tube a bit like a bulb produces lots of X-rays when electricity goes through it.

1 Workers put luggage on a **conveyor belt**. This is a wide loop of rubber that moves all the time. It passes luggage through the scanner.

5 A computer changes information from the sensors into an image of what is inside the luggage.

This is how a luggage scanner works.

It takes time and **effort** to carry luggage around large **terminals**. Some **machines**, such as luggage carts, help people and their belongings get around more easily. It takes less effort for passengers to push a **load** on wheels than to drag it along the ground.

Electric carts carry people who cannot walk very well through terminals.

Know where to go

Signs and screens help people find their way around. Some signs have large letters, such as EXIT. Others show gate numbers, where different planes are waiting. Some signs have symbols. Symbols give information without using words or numbers. For example, signs for bathrooms have a picture of a man or woman.

Flight information

Screens in a terminal show flight information and can change by the minute. They tell passengers which gate their plane will leave from and whether a flight is delayed.

Passengers get the flight information they need from display boards like this.

AT WORK

MINISCREENS

Information display boards are made up of many small screens, similar to those on mobile phones. A single number or letter fits on each screen. Flight information such as destinations or departure or arrival times appear on the boards when different screens light up together.

MOVING WHILE STANDING

The travelator, or moving walkway, is like an escalator that moves flat on the ground. A travelator can carry many passengers over long distances at the same time. People can stand still or walk normally on a travelator. Either way they use less **effort** to move faster!

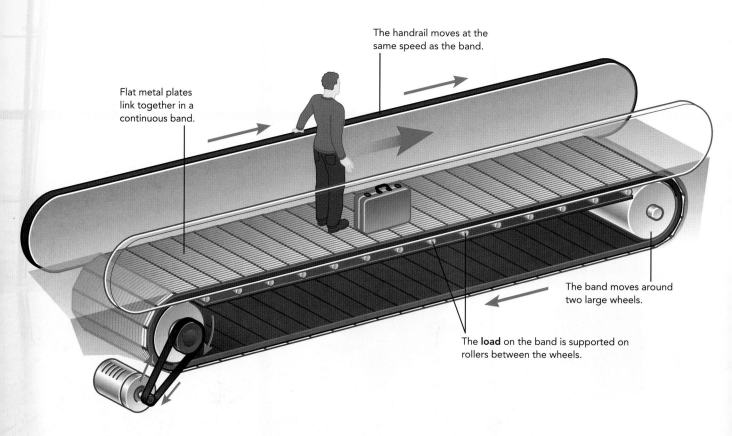

The handrail moves at the same speed as the band.

Flat metal plates link together in a continuous band.

The band moves around two large wheels.

The **load** on the band is supported on rollers between the wheels.

Passengers can also set their luggage on a travelator so they don't have to carry it.

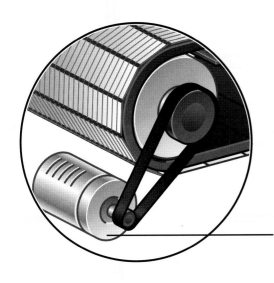

An **electric motor** makes the wheels turn,which pulls the band around. At any time half of the band has people on it and half is underneath the travelator.

A MOVING PAVEMENT

The travelator at Montparnasse Metro station in Paris moves at the speed of an average city bus! The French call it the *trottoir roulant rapide*, which means fast rolling pavement. You have to be careful when you get on that you don't fall over. Many people think these moving pavements might be the way we get around in big cities in the future.

FLYING MACHINES

You see different types of **aircraft** on an airport **runway**. There are big passenger jets that can carry hundreds of people and their luggage over long distances. There are smaller airplanes that carry fewer people over shorter distances, and sometimes there are helicopters, too.

These airplanes are lining up at the end of a runway, waiting for their turn to take off into the sky.

AT WORK

STAYING IN THE SKY

Everything on Earth is pulled toward the ground by the **force** of **gravity**. Because their wings create an upward push or **lift** when they fly forward, airplanes do not fall from the sky. Most airplane wings are curved on top and flatter underneath. As this special wing shape moves through air, it pushes the air downward. The air pushes back and creates lift.

Spinning blades

Helicopters have several blades shaped like narrow wings called a **rotor**. The rotor creates a downward push against air when it spins. This makes the helicopter rise up.

The rotor at the back gives a sideways push to keep the helicopter from twisting around as the big rotor spins.

JETS IN THE SKY

Passenger jets weigh hundreds of tons. They need a very big thrust, or forward push, to move fast enough to create **lift**. Most have two or four powerful turbojet **engines** attached to their wings to do the work.

The two turbojet engines on this airplane draw air in and make it lift.

AT WORK

BIGGEST PLANE
The A380 Airbus is the biggest passenger jet in the world. It has a tail the height of a seven-story building and its wings are big enough to park 70 cars on!

Hot gases exploding out of the back
of a jet engine make it fly forward.

A large fan with lots of angled
blades spins to suck cool air
into the engine

Fuel pipe

Cold air and hot gases blowing backward
from the engine push the engine forward.
This creates thrust.

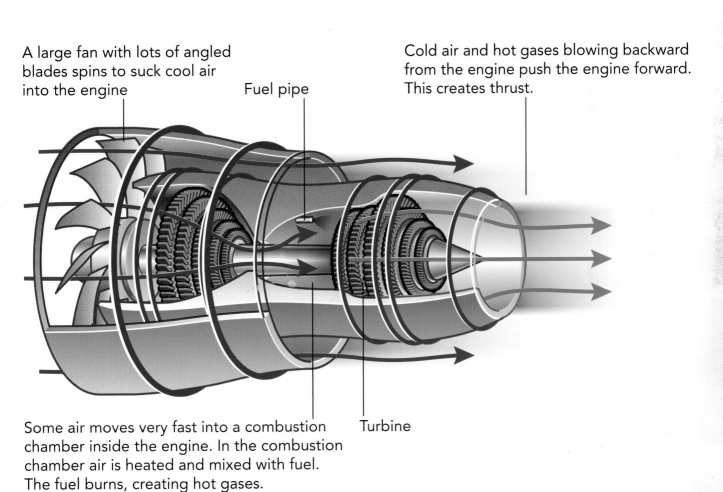

Some air moves very fast into a combustion
chamber inside the engine. In the combustion
chamber air is heated and mixed with fuel.
The fuel burns, creating hot gases.

Turbine

HELP ON THE GROUND

There are many **machines** besides **aircraft** on the **apron** of the airport. Some help passengers get onto airplanes. Buses carry passengers from the **terminal**. Stairs on wheels move next to the aircraft to help people get on and off.

Care and repair

Airplanes are stored in large sheds called hangars. When workers fix engines or repaint planes inside hangars, they often stand on platforms raised by scissor lifts.

Scissor lift

The worker presses buttons to make a motor close up the bottom levers of the scissor lift. This raises the working platform.

AT WORK

SCISSORS AT WORK

A pair of scissors is a simple machine made of two metal **levers** joined at a point called the **fulcrum**. Moving the levers apart on one side of the fulcrum opens the other ends. It also shortens how far the levers reach. A scissor lift works like several pairs of scissors stacked and attached together.

Towing planes

Tow tractors move heavy airplanes when their **engines** are turned off. Tow tractors are like long trailers. Most tow tractors pull the plane by its front wheels. Some raise up and then rest the nose (front) of the aircraft on their back and drag the aircraft along!

This tow tractor is much smaller than the Airbus A340-600 it is dragging along!

HELP IN THE AIR

Some of the most important workers at an airport are responsible for air traffic control. Their job is to direct **aircraft** on the ground and in the air. Air traffic control is based in a tall building called the control tower.

Controlling the air

Air traffic controllers use **machines** to see where different airplanes are in the sky and where they are heading. They use this information to make maps of air traffic on computers. Workers talk to pilots in airplanes using radios. They instruct pilots to fly at a safe distance from each other. This is usually at least 5.5 miles (9 kilometers) behind each other, and 1,000 feet (300 meters) above each other. Controllers also tell pilots when the runway is clear so they can land safely.

AT WORK

WEATHER ALERT

It is not safe to land airplanes when there are heavy storms or high winds. Airplanes usually fly high above clouds, so they cannot tell what the weather is like near land. Air traffic control always has the latest weather forecasts for the area around their airport so they can keep airplanes away from bad weather.

From the air traffic control tower there is a good view of the runway and the sky above the airport.

SEEING PLANES IN THE SKY

Air traffic controllers cannot see **aircraft** when it is dark, when weather is bad, or when a plane is high up. So they use radar to track aircraft. Radar **machines** send out **radio waves** and detect any that bounce off aircraft to figure out the position of the planes.

Information sent and received by radars help workers know which planes are in the air and exactly where they are.

AT WORK

LONG-DISTANCE CONTROL

Air traffic controllers are responsible for a lot of air space. Some radars can spot aircraft up to 230 miles (370 kilometers) away!

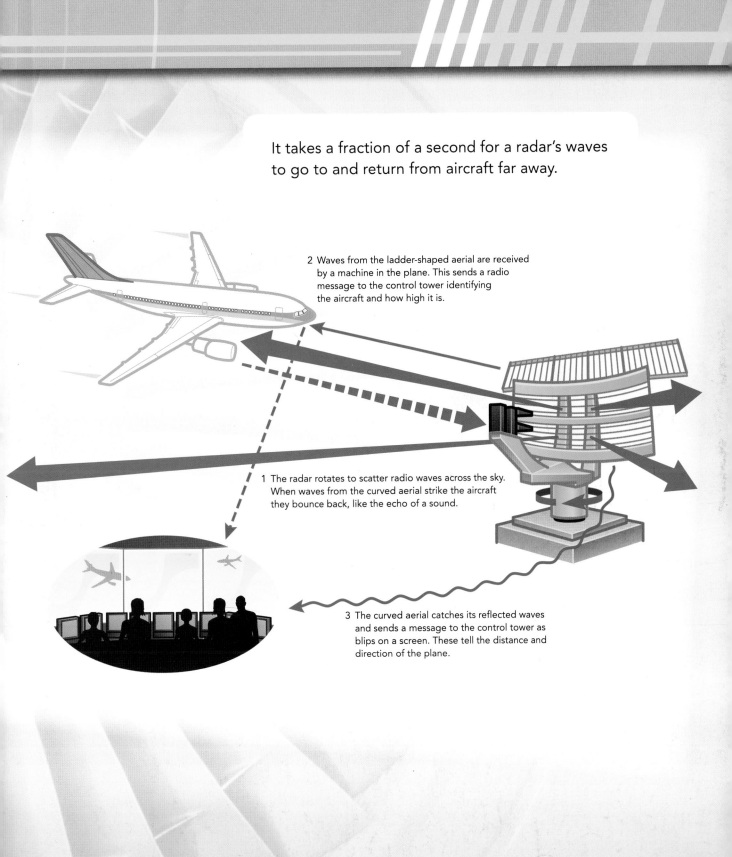

It takes a fraction of a second for a radar's waves to go to and return from aircraft far away.

2 Waves from the ladder-shaped aerial are received by a machine in the plane. This sends a radio message to the control tower identifying the aircraft and how high it is.

1 The radar rotates to scatter radio waves across the sky. When waves from the curved aerial strike the aircraft they bounce back, like the echo of a sound.

3 The curved aerial catches its reflected waves and sends a message to the control tower as blips on a screen. These tell the distance and direction of the plane.

TOUCH DOWN

Airplanes take off from and land on special wide roads called **runways**. Runways can get very busy. It takes about two minutes for an airplane to touch down and drive off the runway before another plane can use it. At big airports there are several runways. Pilots need to know which one to use and also where it is at the airport. Imagine how tricky it must be to find a runway at night!

The runway lights are controlled by workers using computers in the control tower.

AT WORK

FOLLOW THE LIGHTS

There are large patterns of lights around runways. Some lights show the pilot how to approach the runway from the air. Others mark the edges of the runway. Some light up when the airplane is flying in at the wrong angle needed to land safely.

Wheels out

The wheels of some airplanes remain folded in its wings or its underbelly during a flight. If the wheels of an airplane stayed down during a flight, air would push on the wheels. This air resistance, or drag, would slow down the airplane. Just before landing, the pilot operates a **machine** that folds the wheels down so they can roll along the runway.

The wheels on the underside of an airplane allow it to roll down the runway after landing.

AIRPORT TECHNOLOGY

Some of the **machines** in airports are very complicated, but many of them use similar technology to do their work.

Technology at airports help people travel long distances safely and quickly.

Bouncing beams

Three machines work by sending out rays or beams and detecting how they reflect, or bounce off, objects:

- The bar code reader uses light rays.

- The luggage **scanner** uses X-rays.

- The radar system uses **radio waves**.

All these machines need computers to turn the information they gather about objects into images we can understand.

Moving loads

Several machines save people **effort** in moving themselves or their **loads**:

- Luggage carts support loads on wheels.

- Travelators and **conveyor belts** in luggage scanners support loads on a moving belt.

- Scissor lifts support and raise loads using **levers**.

Light patterns

Some airport machines create light patterns to display information:

- Display screens show passengers whether airplanes are on time, and which gates they need to go to.

- Patterns of lights on a **runway** show pilots where to land.

Escalators are another type of machine that move people and other loads at an airport.

Angled blades

Moving a blade quickly at an angle makes air push in different ways:

- Wings and **rotors** on **aircraft** move fast through air to create **lift**.

- Fans on turbojet **engines** push air inside. Then the fuel burns faster and pushes hot gases out.

GLOSSARY

aircraft vehicle for traveling through air. Planes and helicopters are types of aircraft.

apron paved surface where aircraft park while not in use. Passengers get in and out of planes on the apron.

cargo things carried by a vehicle. On a passenger plane the cargo is mostly luggage.

conveyor belt moving belt that transports objects. A conveyor belt has a continuous loop of material that keeps turning.

effort use of energy. It takes effort to push a wheelbarrow or use a hammer.

electric motor machine that uses electrical energy to make machines move

energy force that makes things work. Some machines are powered by electrical energy.

engine machine that uses fuel to create movement. An aircraft engine provides the power for taking off, landing, and flying.

force pushing or pulling action. We use a pushing force to make carts work.

fulcrum support or point on which a lever rests

gravity invisible force that pulls everything toward the Earth. When you throw a ball, gravity is what makes it fall to the ground.

hold cargo area. On a plane the hold is where cargo such as luggage is stored.

lever simple machine that helps lift loads. A see-saw is a type of lever.

lift upward push. An airplane uses lift to act against gravity and stay in the air.

load weight that has to be moved or lifted. A backpack of school books is a type of load.

machine device that helps us do work. Hammers are machines that help us pound nails into wood.

magnet piece of iron or other material that produces a magnetic force. This force makes magnets attract other metals.

magnetic field area around a magnet where the magnetic force works. A magnetic field is strongest at the ends of a bar magnet.

radio waves invisible rays of energy that travel through air. Radio waves carry information for TVs and radios.

rotor rotating blades of a helicopter. The back rotor keeps helicopters flying upright.

runway wide road at an airport. Aircraft use runways for taking off and landing.

scanner electronic device that can read codes or see inside things. Airport scanners use X-rays to see inside suitcases.

security something that protects us from danger or loss. Airport security workers use machines to make sure that bags do not contain weapons.

sensor device that senses light or other signals and produces an electronic signal from them. Some light sensors can determine when it is dark and turn lights on.

terminal area of an airport. Planes load or unload passengers or goods at an airport terminal.

FIND OUT MORE

Books

Bingham, Caroline. *Airplane (Machines at Work)*.
New York: DK Publishing, 2006.

Humphrey, Paul. *At the Airport (Reading Roundabout)*.
New York:Franklin Watts Ltd., 2006.

West, David. *Plane (Why Things Don't Work)*.
Chicago: Raintree, 2006.

Websites

www.boeing.com/companyoffices/aboutus/kids/
This site has games and activities. You can also link to their "wonder of flight" pages. There you can find out more about how things fly and the history of flight.

www.faa.gov/education_research/education/student/resources/ kids_corner
The Federal Aviation Administration's Kid's Corner features aviation games, experiments, and links to aviation technology and history websites.

www.pbs.org/kcet/chasing thesun/timeline/2000.html
A timeline of aviation from 1900 through present day.

INDEX